Above All,

Guard Your Edges

A Girl's Guided Journal to Reducing the Effects
of Stress

Eunice Mingo Blakely

DEDICATION

This book is dedicated to all of my sisters who are moving from just surviving to THRIVING.
May your edges continue grow and forever GLOW!

TABLE OF CONTENTS

ACKNOWLEDGMENTS

I would like to express my sincere gratitude to Myi Baker and my MyiMindBuilder Sisters for the hard push and encouragement to get this challenge completed. It has given me the courage to do something I have wanted to do a very long time. Write and Share!

I would also like to thank my mother and sister for encouraging me to continue to create and give my gift to the world. Special thanks to my son, "Tank" who has always been my Number 1 fan. I cannot forget my loving friends who give their support in more ways than I can begin to say. I appreciate the love, valuable insight and constructive feedback given by each and every one of you.

INTRODUCTION

As the saying goes, "anything buried alive never dies." Any negativity growing and breeding within our bodies will not yield positive results. Different people have different responses to stress. One of the most rampant physical effects of stress and anxiety is hair loss. Another one is weight loss or gain but we will deal with that later. The purpose of this creative tool is to get you to dig deep and pull out parts of yourself you may need to drop. Self-reflection and becoming fully self-aware is not for the faint at heart. It is work. While some parts of growth can be challenging, the euphoric feeling that comes with overcoming obstacles is astounding. You were meant to do more than just survive; you were destined to Thrive! Getting to the heart of ourselves, releasing toxins and living intentionally are great action steps toward reducing the stress in our lives.

Journaling is an extremely therapeutic tool. The purpose is to get what's on the inside, up and out. No worries about the length of your writing, Do You. Just make sure you are responding to the prompt as honestly as you can. Also, journal when it is best for you. Some journal best upon rising, while others do better prior to bed. If midday is your thing, then do that. There is no right or wrong way when it comes to doing you. No need to complete these prompts in any certain order. Some of the following journal prompts may be a little heavy; meaning they will stir up some buried emotions. Other prompts may be fun and will inspire you to create new exciting experiences. Some prompts were added to be repeated more often than others. Before writing, always take a few moments to breathe in and out at least three times. If you need to stop while in the middle of a prompt and breathe, please do. Be Careful with You! Again, this is your journal, you make the rules!

FROM THE AUTHOR

This journal comes as a result of a time in my life where I experienced hardships, heartbreaks, disappointments, anxiety and depression simultaneously; on a daily basis. I was working in the behavioral health field as a director in a local primary care agency and experiencing all kinds of havoc, bullying and unfair treatment in the workplace.

I was anxious and depressed at the same time. Either I couldn't sleep or I slept too much. I felt like I was under the gun at my job and in my personal life. Deadlines to beat and expectations to meet began to take a toll on me. I found myself with an irregular heartbeat, bad nerves and a feeling of impending doom all the time. On top of ALL of that, I started to lose my hair. At first I did not notice this because I kept a short cut. But then it happened; I noticed the sides of my hair starting to shed; FAST. There was no known cause but stress. Girl, I had lost almost all of my edges.

I wrote this journal to help other successful women understand the power in being painfully honest with themselves. We must address the old, the buried, the unacknowledged and the new pains in our lives because it affects us from the inside out. We must grow through what we go through. This is how you avoid losing your edges! Sisters, always be willing to explore positions, thoughts, feelings and beliefs that may contribute to current stressors; even the hard stuff. It's time to get back in the driver's seat and take control. I know you are ready for the ride!

\LET's SNATCH THESE EDGES/

DAY 1

LET'S GET STARTED!

Stress affects our lives in multiple ways. It disturbs us mentally, physically, spiritually, and emotionally. Moving through life without accepting what's really going on around you is extremely hazardous. Avoiding what you need to deal with causes even more strain on your mental well-being. In order to move to a more peaceful space, an acknowledgment of the pressures in your life must come first.

Edge Control

Make a list of the top three things that are causing you stress right now. Think about possible solutions to these problems and write them down as well. Breathe.

1.

2.

3.

Solutions:

_____

_____

JOURNAL

*Struggle does not always have
to be a part of your story.*

DAY 2

IT'S A PROCESS

The way we process and handle stressors, significantly determines how we are affected. We, unintentionally, internalize things and stuff them in different places within us. This is often done as a survival mechanism and can prove to be extremely harmful. Although we may not feel consumed by the stressor, we must realize that our body is keeping score. Nothing within goes unnoticed. Ever. It affects you. Getting something that has been buried, out, can have you feeling all kinds of ways. Self-care exercises like taking a walk, deep breathing, or taking a bath with your favorite essential oil, will help you move through those tough moments.

Edge Control

Is there anything that you have been avoiding, or have stuffed because it was too difficult to deal with? Explore why you avoid certain situations. Write out the top three things you're avoiding & the relief you would feel if you found the courage to tackle them head-on.

continued on next page

IT'S A PROCESS

1.I'm avoiding _____

The relief I would get if I tackled:

_____

_____

2. I'm avoiding _____

The relief I would get if I tackled:

_____

_____

3. I'm avoiding _____

The relief I would get if I tackled:

_____

_____

JOURNAL

_____

_____

_____

_____

_____

_____

_____

_____

_____

_____

FORGIVE & FORGET

People often say, "I will forgive but I won't forget." Although this is a common statement, it's not the healthiest way to live. My response to this is usually the same every time – it is almost impossible to forget something significant unless you have amnesia or some other medical condition; so, each time you remember the offense, it's time to forgive again. It's more important to learn the lesson than holding it against someone for life. Release it, and them, if need be. Forgiveness is not something we do for others, it's something we do for ourselves. It's emotional freedom.

Edge Control

Write at least one thing you want to forgive someone for but you can't move past it. Write about something you want to forgive yourself about. If you're past this point, write about a time when you exercised forgiveness, or when someone forgave you. How did you feel?

I forgive _____ for _____

continued on next page

DAY 3 (CON'T)

FORGIVE & FORGET

I forgive myself for

_____

_____

_____

JOURNAL

The Serenity Prayer

God grant me the serenity

To accept the things I cannot change;

Courage to change the things I can;

And wisdom to know the difference.

Living one day at a time;

Enjoying one moment at a time;

Accepting hardships as the pathway to peace;

Taking, as He did, this sinful world

As it is, not as I would have it;

Trusting that He will make things right

If I surrender to His Will;

So that I may be reasonably happy in this life

And supremely happy with Him

Forever and ever in the next.

Amen

Reinhold Niebuhr

DAY 4

SERENITY

The realization that some problems may not have a solution within our power, can be overwhelming. This awareness usually comes after investing countless hours of physical and emotional energy. In this case, learning, and practicing, ACCEPTANCE is instrumental. If you're familiar with the Serenity Prayer, there is a part that encourages us to, "accept the things we cannot change." Coming to a place of acceptance can be a difficult process, as well as, developing the courage to accept what is. Release the negative energy associated with it, and trust that your Higher Power has already taken care of it. Acceptance is key.

Edge Control

Write about a situation that bothers you, yet, it would seem like there's absolutely nothing you can do about it.

I accept that I cannot change _____

and now, I release _____
and the negative energy that came with it.

I accept that I cannot change _____
and now, I release and the negative energy that came with it. I now move forward.

Journal about the things you can change.

JOURNAL

_____

_____

_____

_____

_____

_____

_____

_____

_____

_____

"If the thought of it brings sorrow to your mind, then by all means place a positive interpretation on it and then switch your focus to what brings you joy."

~ Edmond Mbi

REFLECT

It is important we start to resolve and release negative feelings each day. It is just as important; to record the happy feelings we experience. Let's take a moment to reflect on the feelings you have experienced throughout your day.

Edge Control

Think about the negative feelings you've experienced today.

Is there a particular event that stood out? If it is a happy feeling you are recording, be sure to look at it often!

How did it make you feel?

_____

_____

Why did it make you feel that way?

_____

_____

Journal about the negative feelings from day 5 and release it.

JOURNAL

_____

_____

_____

_____

_____

_____

_____

_____

_____

_____

"He who get upset about you setting boundaries are the ones who were benefiting from you having none."

- Unknown

DAY 6

BOUNDARIES

Are you a person that has a problem saying NO to people? Do you dream of saying YES more? Think about this for a moment. Choose the one that suits you best. Saying NO does not make you mean, or rude. It means you honor yourself by setting boundaries in your life. People who love and honor you will respect the boundaries you set. Saying YES to the things YOU desire in life will help you to overcome fears and build more memorable moments.

Edge Control

Write a list of things you should start saying NO to today.

What would you like to start saying YES to? Make a list!

I will say no to:

_____

I will say YES to:

_____

JOURNAL

_____

_____

_____

_____

_____

_____

_____

_____

_____

_____

"In a world full of game players, the only way to set yourself apart is to be a game changer."

~ Matshona Dhliwayo

DAY 7

BE YOU

Many adults and children are often described as weird. Honestly, I have been called weird once, maybe twice, or three times. Although there is no such thing as normal, the world, sometimes, has its own idea of what is considered the norm. The things that make you different and stand out from the crowd are really gifts. Embrace that you are a Designer's Original and there is only one you.

Edge Control

What are some characteristics that make you unique?

_____

_____

_____

continued on next page

46

BE YOU

Write about how you will embrace and honor who you are; just the way you are. Start your sentences off with "**I will.....**"

_____

_____

_____

JOURNAL

"Asking for help is never a sign of weakness. It's one of the bravest things you can do. And it can save your life."

~ Lily Collins,

DAY 8

IT'S OK TO ASK FOR HELP

Life is not meant to be done alone. Having a supportive Tribe, or Circle will help you navigate the most trying times while celebrating your wins. Make a commitment to lean on your tribe when you need to. Love, value, and include them. Make a promise to call, email, or text your tribe when something new or exciting happens in your world. Make efforts to ensure you keep loving, compassionate and sober-minded people around you.

Edge Control

Make a list of the people who support you during your good and bad moments.

_____

_____

_____

continued on next page

DAY 8 (CON'T)

IT'S OK TO ASK FOR HELP

Write down the ways you feel they can play more significant roles in the exciting moments of your life.

_____

_____

JOURNAL

_____

_____

_____

_____

_____

_____

_____

_____

_____

_____

*"Give space to your thoughts,
clear the noise in your head,
chit-chat with your inner critic,
decide and move on."*

~Cristina Imre

DAY 9

LOVE YOURSELF

The relationship you have with yourself is the most important relationship you will ever have. The conversations you have with yourself can determine the level of success and happiness you experience. Some of us have a vocal critic that lives within us. Think about the times when your inner critic has been a hindrance. Think about how you would encourage someone else who you heard saying those same things about themselves. Make a choice to tell your Inner Critic to SHUT UP so you can move forward! Tell the same to your outside critics as well. Remember, you do more things right than you do wrong.

Edge Control

Write out what your inner critic says to you. Write a replacement thought for each thing your inner critic says.

My inner critic says:

1._____

2._____

3._____

continued on next page

DAY 9 (CON'T)

LOVE YOURSELF

My replacement thoughts are:

1._____

2._____

3._____

JOURNAL

"If you are living an original life, there is absolutely no need to compete with anyone else."

~ Edmond Mbiaka

BE YOUR ONLY COMPETITION

Have you ever noticed someone competing against you and you did not know there was even a contest? People often get into competition with others without realizing it. Sometimes that person may be you. If it is, you are adding more stress and pressure to your life than you realize. This is not healthy, and probably is a downplay of your true abilities. You will never fully operate with your gift by using someone else's measuring stick. Be You. You are enough!

Edge Control

Let's explore this more. Do you sometimes compare yourself to others?

_____

_____

What will it take for you to be fulfilled based on your own standards?

_____

_____

_____

You can never lose by choosing to be better than the person you were yesterday.

JOURNAL

_____

_____

_____

_____

_____

_____

_____

_____

Imposter Syndrome is feeling like

you're a fraud, and you don't actually deserve your job and accomplishments.

DAY 11

DON'T SHRINK

There are times in life where we doubt our talents, skills, and abilities. Everyone does it. We minimize our accomplishments and sometimes just refuse to accept compliments. The Inner Critic can often take over and downright win! Although you have some grand accomplishments, do you still ever feel like you haven't done much? This is a sign you may have the Imposter Syndrome. The presence of some self-doubt is normal to an extent, but too much of it is fear-based and increases anxiety levels. The effects of Imposter Syndrome can be reversed. Accept that you are more than enough and you get better every day. Overcome your doubts and be your biggest fan.

Edge Control

Let's write about some of your successes, accomplishments, etc…

What are some of your successes or accomplishments?

_____

_____

continued on next page

DON'T SHRINK

How did you feel?

_____

Write about a task you would like to complete, be it large or small.

I would like to complete:

_____

_____

Celebration is important! Make a short list of ways you will celebrate each achievement.

_____

_____

JOURNAL

"There's a reason why the rear-view mirror is so small, and the windshield is so big because where you're headed is much more important than what you've left behind."

Joel Olsten

DAY 12

OLD HABITS DIE HARD

It's quite amazing when we think about some of the patterns or habits we have developed. Some of them we've picked up along the way, while others may have been acquired for protection or as a form of defense mechanism. Either way, we realize some of the ways we do things are not conducive for our own growth. The same goes for relationship patterns. Some are just familiar and comfortable. Although old habits die hard, they can be conquered, when replaced by heightened awareness and new actions. Make the decision to do a new thing. Don't fall back into old patterns of living just because it feels familiar. You left them behind because you wanted better for yourself. It is impossible to move forward and backward at the same time.

Edge Control

What unhealthy habit, relationship, or behavior pattern do you need to let go?

_____

_____

continued on next page

84

DAY 12 (CON'T)

OLD HABITS DIE HARD

What is a better alternative and why?

_____

_____

_____

_____

JOURNAL

Journal about new patterns you want to form and how you want to feel when they are in place.

_____

_____

_____

_____

_____

_____

_____

_____

"Give, and you will receive.

Your gift will return to you in full—pressed down, shaken together to make room for more, running over, and poured into your lap. The amount you give will determine the amount you get back."

Luke 6:38

GIVE BACK, FULFILL OTHERS

Pouring into others can have a positive impact on your own self-esteem. Our talents and unique gifts are not for us to keep within ourselves, but to give, freely, to others. One part of being a good steward is knowing when to give freely. Remember to maintain balance. You are responsible for keeping your cup full, so you can give from the overflow.

Edge Control

Write about the time(s), that you have made a positive impact on someone else. How did this make you feel?

_____

_____

How did it change them for the better?

_____

_____

How did this make you feel?

_____

_____

JOURNAL

Journal about ways you will make a conscious effort to share your gift with others.

_____

_____

_____

_____

_____

_____

_____

_____

_____

"Where the Mind Goes, the Body Follows-

Perception precedes action"

Ryan Holiday

DECLUTTER

I know we have all heard the slogan, "A mind is a terrible thing to waste." Our minds are incredibly delicate, and must be renewed EVERYDAY; sometimes, several times a day. Your mind should not be a place of clutter; declare it as a place where good thoughts dwell. Your mind should not be wandering aimlessly; decree that you have control over your thoughts. Daydreaming is not good when it interferes with your productivity. It's a time waster. Don't allow your thoughts to control you.

Edge Control

What's on your mind most of the time?

_____

_____

_____

_____

continued on next page

DAY 14 (CON'T)

DECLUTTER

What are your thoughts centered on?

_____

_____

_____

Where is your focus?

_____

_____

_____

JOURNAL

Journal about how you will shift your focus when you
find thoughts out of alignment

_____

_____

_____

_____

_____

_____

_____

_____

_____

You cannot make sound decisions if you are not on one accord-

mind, body and spirit.

IT FORMS IN THE MIND

Clearing your mind can be a rigid process. There are levels to this mind-thing and the clutter is real! When we house so many negative feelings and experiences in our hearts, it alters the way we process our thoughts. The refusal to deal with the issues of life leads to us becoming misguided by destructive emotions. We literally can become ill. Your mind is not a Toxic Waste Dump. If all you house in there is junk, anger, resentments, malice, and hurt; your actions will be as such. Only a sound mind makes good decisions. You cannot be on one accord of Mind, Body, and Soul if all you're carrying around is junk.

Edge Control

Think about whether you have any mind or heart clutter that needs to get purged.

What toxic emotions do you have that needs to be dumped?

_____

_____

continued on next page

DAY 15 (CON'T)

IT FORMS IN THE MIND

Do you have moods that are controlled by negative thoughts and feelings?

Replace negative thoughts with positive affirmations.

Negative Thought:

_____

Positive Thought or Affirmation:

_____

Negative Thought:

_____

Positive Thought or Affirmation:

_____

Negative Thought:

_____

Positive Thought or Affirmation:

_____

JOURNAL

"Your feelings will change based on your experiences, but do not let them harden your heart."

~Unknown

THE FEELS

There are times in life when you will have to tell your feelings how to feel by Faith. This is part of employing those self-management skills we discussed earlier. In this aspect, I am referring to managing your feelings. Feelings are fickle and can change at any moment based on the circumstances. Never give in to feelings of inferiority, depression, poor self-worth, etc.... Believe and know that things will get better and feelings are temporary. You must make it a practice to stop when you need to and then move through your feelings.

Edge Control

What negative feelings do you find yourself entertaining most?

_____

_____

_____

continued on next page

DAY 16 (CON'T)

THE FEELS

How often do you hear the negative chatter in your mind?

_____

_____

Make a list of those negative thoughts and feelings. Underneath each negative thought, write your replacement thought and highlight it in your favorite color.

_____

_____

_____

_____

Declare and decree that IT IS SO!

JOURNAL

*"The secret of getting ahead is getting started. The secret of getting started is breaking your complex, overwhelming **tasks** into small **manageable tasks**, and then starting on the first one."*

~Mark Twain

DUMP IT

There are times when our heads can be so crowded, that it hurts to even think. During these times, it can be useful to do a brain dump. A brain dump is getting all your thoughts OUT of your brain and onto paper. This release, literally, serves as an act of facing what's in front of you. It's creating a game plan for everything that causes anxiety, thinking distortions, worries, etc. Whatever it is, just get it out. Give yourself permission to let it go. Once you have made the dump, come back to the dumpsite with a clear head and then make decisions. Don't let it drive you insane. Make tasks manageable so they can be completed.

Edge Control

Identify a special notebook to serve as your official dumpsite.

What pressing thoughts do you have right now? Take some time and do a Brain Dump right now, then, clean it up later.

_____

_____

JOURNAL

_____

_____

_____

_____

_____

_____

_____

_____

_____

_____

"If you don't love yourself, you'll always be chasing after people who don't love you either."

Mandy Hale

THE NEED TO LOVE & BE LOVED

One of the greatest needs we have as humans is to love and be loved. It's instinctive. Love is something we must be clear about. Knowing how to receive and give love are crucial parts of sustaining any relationship, especially the one with yourself. You cannot expect someone else to know how to love you if you are unclear about it yourself.

Edge Control

How do you define love?

_____

_____

How would you like love displayed to you?

_____

_____

In what ways do you show love?

_____

_____

JOURNAL

She is willing to compromise on most things, but respect, honesty and loyalty are non-negotiable.

Unknown

DAY 19

NEGOTIABLES & NON-NEGOTIABLES

The way we relate to others is a very important aspect of life. We must learn to take care of ourselves first before we enter any type of relationship. This is not selfishness, it is wisdom. Learn about you, first. Heal your wounds, so that you will not bring injury to someone else. More importantly, learn what is tolerable for you and how you will handle red flags when you see them. Having potential and love alone will never sustain any relationship. Make sure you know the qualities you desire to see in a mate. By the same token, be even more clear about what you will not tolerate in any relationship.

Edge Control

How do you communicate your needs?

_____

_____

_____

continued on next page

NEGOTIABLES & NON-NEGOTIABLES

Is this way effective? What adjustments can you make?

_____

_____

What's negotiable and non-negotiable in your
  relationships?

_____

_____

_____

What will you say, and do, when you see red
flags?

_____

_____

_____

JOURNAL

Edge Control

So far, we have done the difficult work of getting our stressors on paper. Give yourself a hand. You have done well. I honor your hard work and I am proud of the steps you've made toward guarding your Edges and learning new ways to live life. BREATHE and give yourself a hug. Now, let's take some time to do some more Edge Control. This Edge Control section contains less complex prompts that will provide practical ways to release everyday stress in your life.

Let's Release and BREATHE.

*"Organizing isn't the goal,
simplifying your life is."*

Unknown

GET IN ORDER

Having some type of order in our lives relieves stress in more ways than we think. Creating a schedule, jotting down a to-do list, sticky notes, electronic calendars, and setting reminders can help reduce anxiety in our lives. Although you may not follow your lists or schedule as written, you will experience a sense of relief knowing what's on your plate. If you failed to prepare, then you were preparing to fail. Being scattered most of the time can make life frustrating, but having a way to organize your day and mind will increase satisfaction.

Edge Control

In what ways do you prepare for the upcoming day, week, month, or year?

_____

_____

_____

_____

continued on next page

144

DAY 20 (CON'T)

GET IN ORDER

How can you create order where there is none?

_____

_____

_____

_____

When do you look at your schedule and how do you make adjustments?

_____

_____

_____

JOURNAL

---

*Happiness, while not a
permanent state, is a more stable
state than pleasure. Happiness
generally sticks around for
longer than a few moments at a
time, whereas pleasure can come
and go in seconds.”*

PositivePsyhology.com

FIND YOUR HAPPY

Think about some of the happy or proud moments you've had in your life. Go as far back as you can remember. It may help if you divide your life into sections, like school-age, adolescence, young adulthood, college, etc..... Smile and enjoy the memory. Enjoy the moment.

Edge Control

Make a list of those happy times and proud moments in your life.

_____

_____

_____

Jot down how this prompt made you feel.

_____

_____

_____

JOURNAL

_____

_____

_____

_____

_____

_____

_____

_____

_____

_____

_____

"Finish each day and be done with it.

You have done what you could. Some blunders and absurdities no doubt crept in; forget them as soon as you can.

Tomorrow is a new day; begin it well and serenely and with too high a spirit to be encumbered with your old nonsense."

~ Ralph Waldo Emerson

DAY 22

DISCOURAGEMENT VS PERSEVERANCE

Living an intentional life involves creating a roadmap for your successes, as well as for your bounce-backs. Having a life plan helps provide you with a blueprint of where you would want to be at different points in your life. While this is a good practice, you must be okay with the fact that even the best plans can sometimes go left. And that's o.k. Keep it Moving.

Edge Control

In five years, what would you like your life to look like?

_____

_____

_____

_____

continued on next page

DAY 22 (CON'T)

DISCOURAGEMENT VS PERSEVERANCE

What would you like to be doing?

_____

_____

_____

What will you be doing in your spare time?

_____

_____

_____

How will you practice self-care?

_____

_____

_____

JOURNAL

"Always make time to celebrate your hard work and accomplishments; no matter how large or small."

DAY 23

~MEMORIES COME ALIVE~
AUTOBIOGRAPHY

We've all had some times in our lives that are noteworthy. From those moments, we learned countless lessons. Have you ever thought that recording those experiences for later reflection would make an interesting read for you? Spend some time reflecting on the most significant and minor moments in your life.

Edge Control

If you had to write the story of your life, what would you title the major chapters? Start reminiscing and writing.

Chapter 1:

_____

Chapter 2:

_____

Chapter 3:

_____

continued on next page

DAY 23 (CON'T)

~MEMORIES COME ALIVE~
AUTOBIOGRAPHY

Chapter 4:

_____

Chapter 5:

_____

Chapter 6:

_____

Chapter 7:

_____

Chapter 8:

_____

Chapter 9:

_____

Chapter 10:

_____

JOURNAL

"Your soul needs time for solitude and self-reflection.

In order to love, lead, heal and create you must nourish yourself first."

~ Linda Joy.

SELF REFLECTION

A good practice to ensure you are growing, and going, in a positive direction is implementing a time for Self-Reflection. This time of analysis includes taking an honest look at yourself on a seasonal or quarterly basis. Although you will review this quarterly, gathering the information, monthly, will help you keep an accurate account. This reflection includes goals achieved, situations you handled well, needed adjustments, and accomplishments.

Edge Control

How will you implement a self-reflection practice in your life?

_____

_____

_____

_____

_____

JOURNAL

Count your garden by the flowers,

never by the leaves that fall;

Count your days by golden hours,

don't remember clouds at all!

Count your nights by stars—

not shadows;

count your life with smiles—

not tears.

And with joy

Count your age by friends, not years.

~Unknown

DAY 25

REMEMBER THE TIMES

When was the last time you did something you enjoyed doing? If it's been a while, take time to think about what you enjoy, and how you can incorporate it into your life this week. Life is too short not to enjoy it. It doesn't take much. Always take some time to do something fun or fulfilling. Make new memories.

Edge Control

Write about the times when you really enjoyed yourself. Was it visiting a friend? Did you enjoy a massage? Was it spending the weekend with your cousins back in the day; laughing at any and everything?

What are your funniest memories?

_____

_____

_____

_____

JOURNAL

"Gratitude turns what we have into enough, and more. It turns denial into acceptance, chaos into order, confusion into clarity...it makes sense of our past, brings peace for today, and creates a vision for tomorrow."

Melody Beattie

DAY 26

MY JOI

Joy or *Joi*, as I call it, costs too much for us to give it all away. *"Joi"* is my niece and she brings our family a lot of funny moments. I love to write about funny things that have been done or said for later reflection. Life is serious enough so it doesn't hurt to always have a plan to be joyful. Start a gratitude jar or journal. Pick out special days or times that you will reflect back on moments that you are grateful for. Go ahead and add your *"reflection"* days to your calendar at least quarterly.

Edge Control

Make a list of ten things or moments you are grateful for. Add to this list as often as possible.

1._____

2._____

3._____

4._____

5._____

continued on next page

DAY 26 (CON'T)

MY JOI

6._____

7._____

8._____

9._____

10._____

When will you reflect on moments that bring you joy?

_____

_____

_____

_____

JOURNAL

_____

_____

_____

_____

_____

_____

_____

_____

_____

_____

_____

"You may be faced with many hardships but do not get discouraged.

Keep your hope alive,

never stop dreaming."

~ Lailah Gifty Akita

DAY 27

SET UP TO WIN

We all experience discouragement or heaviness at some time or another. This weight is heavy and can be an extremely difficult process. It causes us to feel tired, drained and defeated. In times like this, we must remind ourselves that something good is in the works. The enemy only attacks progress and attempts to throw us off our games by attacking our thoughts and feelings. Although you may feel wounded and broken, you cannot give up. Let that pain and pressure propel you into your victory as you continue to pursue peace in your mind, heart and soul.

Edge Control

Think about a time when you've felt low, discouraged or defeated.

How long does it usually last?

_____

Does it hinder your progress at work and home?

_____

continued on next page

DAY 27 (CON'T)

SET UP TO WIN

Let's change the narrative here.

If the same or similar scenario(s) happened again, how can you change your reaction to it?

_____

_____

In what ways can you rejuvenate your mind and spirit?

_____

_____

Write three affirmations or scriptures to help uplift and push you through the moment.

1._____

2._____

3._____

JOURNAL

"Either push your limits or suffocate in your comfort zone."

~Arun Purang

DAY 28

BREAK OUT

Remember your worth every day. Stand in your truth. Remaining in places and situations we don't fit in ultimately will damage your view of yourself and your overall outlook on life. Oppression has never been healthy in any situation. You were not born to be in a situation that prevents you from blooming and thriving.

Edge Control

Write the people, places or things that cause you to feel limited or oppressed.

_____

_____

_____

_____

_____

_____

DAY 28 (CON'T)

BREAK OUT

How has your creativity and sense of joy been limited by this oppression?

_____

_____

_____

What will you do to feel more celebrated?

_____

_____

_____

JOURNAL

Don't Stop-
Get It, Get It!

Uncle Luke

DAY 29

ALWAYS TRY AGAIN

Think about how your life would be if you had not tried to do certain things. Think about times when you have been your own worst critic. Being hard on yourself will only keep you in the negative and increase stress. When you choose to think more about the times you tried and succeeded, you will begin to change the outlook you have on yourself and your life as a whole. Adopt the outlook that there are no failures, only lessons learned. Don't be the one to stop you from living your best life.

Edge Control

Make a list of feelings you felt when you tried and did well.

_____

_____

Write about the consequence of not trying.

_____

_____

continued on next page

209

DAY 29 (CON'T)

ALWAYS TRY AGAIN

Write about three occurrences in your life you perceive as failure?

1._____

2._____

3._____

What did you learn?

_____

_____

_____

How can these lessons help you toward living your best, blessed life?

_____

_____

JOURNAL

*Be careful how you treat
yourself-*

*Be careful how you speak
when experiencing tough
times-*

*Be careful of the people you
chose to be in close
relationship with-*

Be careful what you tolerate-

*Be careful how you handle
your powerful, precious
energy-*

*Be careful with the people you
love.*

*Always move toward what's
good for you and to you.*

Always

Be Careful with You!

~Eunice C. Mingo

DAY 30

BE CAREFUL WITH YOU!

We all can use a little pick me up every now and then. As a matter of fact, it may be a wise practice to encourage ourselves well before we begin to feel discouraged. Even when you are feeling most confident, it is good to encourage yourself by saying "Girl, you got this" or "Yes! I did that." Be your biggest fan in all facets of life. Treat your whole self well. Engage in activities and thoughts that push you toward growth and evoke good vibrations all of the time. You are succeeding in more areas than you are not. Celebrate that!

Edge Control

Meditate on your Life -- Mind, Body and Soul.

How often are you encouraging yourself?

_____

_____

_____

continued on next page

DAY 30 (CON'T)

BE CAREFUL WITH YOU!

What do you need more of?

_____

_____

What do you do you need less of?

_____

_____

_____

What steps will you take to make necessary changes within the next 30 days?

_____

_____

_____

Nobody will ever take care of you better than you. Make sure you are doing a great job.

JOURNAL

SIS,

When you have completed these exploratory exercises, you should have several action plans for different life events. Changing the way you respond to stressors, and other negative situations when they arise is a way to ensure you are not acting-out, based on toxic experiences.

The power of releasing and taking each day as it comes will reduce the anxiety. In turn, we keep our edges tamed, controlled and present. Always take an honest look at your life, be real with yourself, ask for help, and incorporate fun into your life. There is no reason to worry. And pray. Just pray. Prayer, good works and good people will move you closer to living your best life.

Eunice